In Search Of

Jeremiah Dixon

(1733-1779)

Surveyor of the Mason-Dixon Line

by

Simon Webb

Published by the Langley Press, Durham, 2014

This book is an abridged version of
The Life and Times of Jeremiah Dixon, Surveyor of the Mason-Dixon Line, by the same author, which is available
as an Amazon Kindle download.

Unless otherwise stated, all pictures are public domain images from Wikimedia Commons, except for photographs of Cockfield today, which were taken by the author. Front page, clockwise from top right: *The Indians Giving a Talk to Colonel Bouquet*, engraving after Benjamin West, 1766; NASA image of the 2012 transit of Venus; 18th century print of an English Admiral's ship. The map on the back cover, with the Mason-Dixon Line marked in red, is A.J. Johnson's 1864 map of Pennsylvania and Maryland.

ISBN: 978-0-9569259-5-4

Also by Simon Webb:

The Life and Times of Jeremiah Dixon,
Surveyor of the Mason-Dixon Line

Gilbert's Tale: The Life and Death
of Thomas Becket

Mary Ann Cotton: Victorian Serial Killer

In Search of The Little Count:
Joseph Boruwlaski, Durham Celebrity

In Search of the Northern Saints

In Search of Bede

For free downloads and more
from the Langley Press, go to:

http://tinyurl.com/lpdirect

To my friend
Heather Cawte

Contents

I. Death By Water

At about seven in the morning of the tenth of January 1761 the frigate *HMS Seahorse* (twenty-four guns) was sailing at a speed of three knots on a south-westerly course, roughly a hundred miles south-west of Start Point in Devon, England. The *Seahorse*'s lookouts spied a sail to the south-east which proved to be the French frigate *Le Grand* (thirty-four guns). The sail seemed to be getting closer, and it was soon clear that the French ship was giving chase.

By 10:45 the *Le Grand* was close enough to be within range of a pistol, and the ships exchanged fire. The engagement, which 'was very obstinate on both sides' continued for over an hour, during which time the *Seahorse* was boarded three times by the Frenchmen. By twelve, the *Le Grand* had had enough. She 'made all the sail she could from us' and though the *Seahorse* gave chase, the *Le Grand* was much faster.

The quotations in the last paragraph are drawn from the journal of one of the *Seahorse*'s two very important passengers: a man called Charles Mason. The other VIP, who either didn't keep a journal, or kept one that is now lost, was Jeremiah Dixon. Dixon was an English Quaker from Cockfield in County Durham, and he is the subject of this little biography. The two Englishmen were on the *Seahorse* as employees of the Royal Society in London, and had been bound for Bengkulu in Sumatra, to observe an astronomical phenomenon called a transit of Venus.

Later, both men would become famous not for their experience of a sea-battle, or for their work observing Venus, but for surveying what became known as the Mason-Dixon

Line, between Pennsylvania and Maryland in North America. The Mason-Dixon Line can stand comparison with Hadrian's Wall, the Great Wall of China and the Berlin Wall as a boundary of great historical significance. It is still regarded as the dividing line between not just two states, but the Southern and Northern United States. The Line also became an important frontier in the American Civil War. One of the most decisive battles of that war was fought just north of the line, in and around Gettysburg, Pennsylvania, in July 1863; a century after Dixon and Mason began to mark out their Line.

If Captain Smith of the *Seahorse* ever had time to get to know Jeremiah Dixon, he may have found him a strange, paradoxical, surprising and contradictory man. Dixon, who would then have been in his late twenties, was a scientist, yet he was also a man with the large, powerful build of a man suited to hard physical work. He was supposed to be a Quaker, and thus a pacifist, yet he wore a red coat and a black tricorn hat that made him look like a British army officer, at least from a distance.

The redness of Dixon's coat and the 'cocked' character of his hat would have offended against the aesthetics of many eighteenth-century Quaker men, who preferred clothes in plain shapes and colours: drab coats with plain buttons and no pleats, and hats with flat brims.

As the *Le Grand* vanished over to horizon, there was no doubt a victory cheer sent up by the crew of the *Seahorse*; but when the crew and passengers were mustered on deck it was found that eleven men had been killed, and thirty-eight injured. In a letter to Charles Morton, secretary of the Royal Society, Mason expressed his fear that many of the wounded would die of their wounds.

The reason why French frigates such as the *Le Grand* were shooting at British ships in 1761 was because that year was one of the years of what historians call the Seven Years' War.

The war, which lasted from 1756-1763, is also known by several other names: the Spaniards call it the 'English War' and the Americans call it the 'French and Indian War'. King Frederick the Great of Prussia, one of Britain's allies in the conflict, called it the 'Petticoat War' because three women; Empress Maria of Austria, Czarina Elizabeth of Russia, and Madame de Pompadour, the French king's mistress, all had a lot of influence on the progress of the conflict.

At first the English called the war 'Pitt's War', after William Pitt the Elder, the dominant British political figure of the time, whose power went far beyond any of his official posts, and who became virtual prime minister during several of the war years.

Pitt had a vision of Britain as all-powerful within Europe, using her undoubted naval supremacy to command the lucrative trade-routes to and from European colonies such as Canada, and the British colonies on the eastern seaboard of what later became the United States.

Because trade with different European states was so widespread, the Seven Years' War became the first world-wide war, fought on every continent except Australia; of which island continent very little was known until James Cook's famous expedition in 1770.

II. A Second Chance

The *Seahorse* was so badly damaged after her engagement with the *Le Grand* that Captain Smith was forced, as Mason says in his journal, to shorten sail 'to repair our rigging; the standing and run ring being much shattered, our 3 lower masts much wounded in several places, the boats and booms tore to pieces, and several shot in our hull'.

These repairs at sea were probably designed to make the *Seahorse* just seaworthy enough to be able to limp to Plymouth, where she went to be patched up properly.

Unfortunately the weather hindered the attempts of the shattered *Seahorse* to get to Plymouth, and on Sunday the eleventh of January she fired a gun and raised the signal for distress (twice). Eventually the *Jason*, a navy ship, sent two boats. A launch from Hamoaze (now the Devonport Dockyard) arrived to take the wounded to hospital.

The *Seahorse* had set off from Spithead at about two in the afternoon of Thursday 8th January 1761, two days before her engagement with the *Le Grand*. As we know, her mission was to carry Charles Mason and Jeremiah Dixon to Bengkulu in Sumatra, a large island in Indonesia, the southern tip of which lies nearly a thousand miles to the north-west of Australia.

Dixon and Mason were going to this place on the other side of the world as astronomers, to observe a transit of Venus: when that planet crosses in front of the sun.

In a letter dated the twenty-fifth of January 1761, Mason acknowledged receipt of a letter from the Royal Society, in which, evidently, the Society had urged Dixon and Mason to continue on their mission as instructed. Mason re-iterated his opinion (which coincided with the opinion 'of some sagatious friends') that it would be impossible for them 'to reach any part by way of the Cape [of Good Hope] proper for making the Observation that will have East Longitude sufficient to be any use to compare with those made at Greenwich and St Helena'.

Mason went on to suggest 'Scanderoon' (now Iskenderun in Turkey) as an alternative destination, 'to which place if the Council of the Royal Society will please to send us, we shall with the greatest Pleasure obey their commands; but shall not proceed from this, to any other Place, where it is impossible for us to perform what the world in general reasonably expect from us; and therefore shall wait for a Line to inform us of their further pleasure'.

Although the letter is couched in the respectful language of the time, appropriate for a man who was being employed by the illustrious Royal Society, it does contain an absolute refusal on Dixon and Mason's part to attempt to reach anywhere east of the Cape of Good Hope in time to see the transit.

In his letter of the fifth of January, Mason stated that 'the ship will scarcely be ready for sea this next week'. It was still not ready at the end of that month. When the Royal Society got wind of Charles and Jeremiah's intention to abandon any place beyond the Cape as a destination, they sent a blistering letter to the two men at Plymouth, which included the words:

'That their refusal to proceed upon this voyage after their having so publickly and notoriously ingaged in it, will be a Reproach to the Nation in General, to the Royal Society in particular, and more especially and fatally to themselves'.

The letter also included a threat to prosecute the pair 'with the utmost Severity of Law'.

By Monday the fifth of February the *Seahorse*, with a fresh captain, was sailing west again, headed for the Cape of Good Hope, this time in company with His Majesty's frigate, the *Brilliant*. Later the *Seahorse* found herself in company with no less than five naval ships, which must have been reassuring, given the dangers of sea-travel in war-time. This business of travelling in convoys was a definite policy for British shipping at the time, and the places where ships could pause for fresh water and other supplies, such as Tenerife and the island of St Helena, were also used as points where convoys could be formed before travelling further.

At about eleven in the morning of the twenty-seventh of April, Dixon's ship 'pass'd between Penguin Island and the Lions Rump and in the afternoon Anchor'd in Table Bay'.

It had taken the *Seahorse* nearly three months to reach her destination, but Dixon and Mason still had over a month to prepare for the transit of Venus, which was not expected until the sixth of June.

III. A Transit of Venus

Dixon and Mason's mission to observe the 1761 transit of Venus was funded by the king and organised by the prestigious Royal Society. The royal grant amounted to eight thousand pounds – equivalent to well over a million pounds, or 1.7 million U.S. dollars today. The British government's interest in the scheme was not entirely born out of scientific curiosity. It was hoped that by accurately recording the transit of Venus from widely-spaced locations on the surface of the earth, scientists would be able to determine more accurately the sun's distance from the earth – a piece of data essential to accurate navigation.

At the Cape, Dixon and Mason set about supervising the building of a small observatory from wood, bricks, board, canvas, putty and tar. The resulting building was sited in the Rosenburg Gardens, on gently sloping land between Table Mountain and False Bay (now called the Concordia Gardens). It was put together by carpenters from the *Seahorse* and by local craftsmen, and was a squat cylinder five and a half feet high and thirteen feet in diameter, topped by a shallow conical roof.

Dixon and Mason's mini observatory cost forty-eight pounds and seven shillings, including materials and labour, but not including the twenty-two shillings paid to the men who moved the instruments from the *Seahorse* to the observatory. In today's money, the observatory would have cost over three and a half thousand pounds, or five and a half thousand US dollars.

Their main clock, a pendulum model made by John Ellicott of London, had to be carefully levelled and firmly fixed into the ground, and couldn't have been moved (or stolen) without difficulty. The observatory also housed a thermometer made by the instrument-maker John Bird, a County Durham man like Dixon, who had probably known Jeremiah for years.

Dixon and Mason expended an amazing amount of time and effort on Ellicott's clock during their stay in Cape Town, simply because they knew the clock couldn't be reliable, although it was one of the most accurate clocks that would have been available to them at the time. They put it on the ground floor of a house near where the observatory was to be built, and set it going on the fourth of May.

When the little observatory was completed, the clock was moved there and set to 'nearly sidereal time', meaning the time according to the stars. The astronomers then set about checking the 'going' or speed of the clock by working out the correct sidereal time: this they did by observing and timing the movement of the star Procyon. They discovered that the clock was slow, losing about two minutes and seventeen seconds 'per day of the stars'.

The clock, and the astronomical observations they made to determine its 'going', were important because the Royal Society expected their agents to report, as near as possible, the time when the transit of Venus started and ended, as well as the times when, for instance, Venus seemed to be stuck just inside the sun, on its way in and out. These times were to be compared to other estimates recorded by other observers, for instance the future Astronomer Royal Nevil Maskelyne, who was supposed to be observing the transit from St Helena.

The astronomers at the Cape were also equipped with two Gregorian reflecting telescopes, and two 'nozels' or eye-pieces with dark glass in them, to allow direct observation of the sun. They also had a helioscope, which in this case means not a telescope designed especially for viewing the sun, but an alternative eye-piece which would cut out much of the glare by presenting the eye with a reflected image of the sun.

Although Dixon and Mason's view of the eclipse of the moon on the eighteenth of May had been 'very clear', the skies over Cape Town on the days and nights before the transit was due alternated between clear and cloudy. If their view of the transit was completely obscured by clouds, they would have had to return to the Royal Society with no new information on that rare phenomenon, and much of the trouble, expense and indeed danger of their journey would have been for nothing.

By the time the sun rose at a quarter to six in the morning of the sixth of June, Venus was already about three and a half hours into her journey across the face of the sun. To make matters worse, the sun rose into a thick haze, then disappeared behind a black cloud. When the Englishmen first spotted Venus, both she and the sun 'were in a great tremour', but this soon ended and Dixon and Mason were able to watch and record most of the transit, which finished when Venus vanished into the blackness surrounding the sun at around eighteen minutes to nine in the morning.

Despite the threat of clouds, the two Englishmen had succeeded in recording the most complete set of measurements of the 1761 transit of Venus to be assembled in the southern hemisphere.

IV. The Dixons of Cockfield

In 1762 Charles Mason was a widower who had not yet re-married after the death of his first wife, Rebekah, at Greenwich in 1759. He was no doubt keen to see his sons, William and Isaac, after his long absence. Whether these boys were in London, or in Charles's home county of Gloucestershire, Mason would have had far less distance to travel than his colleague Jeremiah Dixon, who had to make the long journey north to the little village of Cockfield in County Durham, to see his own family again.

Dixon never married, but he may have fathered children, though probably not by 1762. The family he would have returned to after his travels to the Cape consisted of, among others, his older brother George, his sister Hannah, another brother called Ralph, and his widowed mother, Mary Dixon, née Hunter. It seems that both Jeremiah and his brother George inherited their intelligence from their mother, who came from Newcastle-upon Tyne and was said to have been the cleverest woman who ever married into the Dixon family.

Jeremiah's father, also called George, had died in 1755, six years before the transit of Venus that would lure his fifth child, and third son, to another hemisphere.

The Dixons had been Quakers since the beginnings of Quakerism in the middle of the seventeenth century, and in Jeremiah's time they attended meeting for worship (the Quaker equivalent of Sunday service) at the nearby village of Raby. Jeremiah's great-grandfather, one of many Georges on the Dixon family tree, was a Quaker in the early days of the sect, and the religious affiliation, like the name George, was passed

15

down through the generations.

Jeremiah probably stayed at Garden House in Cockfield when he visited his home village. This house, which is still standing, was the home that Jeremiah's brother George, as the oldest surviving son, had inherited from their father.

It was here, no doubt lit by a very good coal fire, that the family listened with great interest to Jeremiah's tales of his travels.

Dixon returned home to Cockfield a celebrity, since something like a craze for the transit of Venus had swept Europe in 1761.

It would be nice to be able to say that the Royal Society chose Jeremiah Dixon as one half of the team that was to represent them at the Cape because of his merit alone, but this would not be entirely true.

As a boy growing up to the south of Durham City, Jeremiah came to know at least three notable scientific gentlemen, including the aforementioned John Bird, instrument-maker, a native of Bishop Auckland.

It is likely that Bird, who had close links to the Royal Society, recommended Dixon as a suitable man to accompany Charles Mason to the Cape.

Although Jeremiah was probably not up against any rival candidates, he did have to endure an interview from the Royal Society, where it seems that he was asked if he had studied mathematics at Oxford or Cambridge.

'At neither place,' he replied.

'Then at what public school did you get your rudiments?'

'At no public school.'

'Then pray tell, at what particular seat of learning did you acquire them?'

'In a pit cabin on Cockfield Fell,' said Jeremiah.

This last answer is perhaps Dixon's most famous utterance,

and it repays careful examination. First, we have to remember that by 'public school', Dixon's questioner would have meant one of the old private boarding-schools of England, the most famous of which is Eton College, founded in 1440. These schools are not 'public' in the modern sense, in that the parents or guardians of most of their pupils have to pay fees.

Although Dixon claims here that he didn't attend a public school, he attended a Mr John Kipling's school at Barnard Castle in County Durham; and since Barnard Castle is about seven miles away from Cockfield, it is likely that Dixon boarded at the school, or had digs nearby, at least some of the time. Kipling's school, which George Dixon also attended, seems to have slipped through the fingers of history, and nothing more is now known about it except that the Dixon brothers attended, and that it was in Barnard Castle. Kipling's wouldn't have qualified as a 'public school' since it was probably founded by Kipling himself, and wouldn't have been as ancient as Eton, Harrow or Rugby.

Dixon's claim that he learned his rudiments 'in a pit-cabin on Cockfield Fell' may reflect his dissatisfaction with Kipling's school, or it may have been a self-deprecating crack in typical Durham style. To the representatives of the Royal Society who first heard it, it might have sounded like a rebuke to their aristocratic ideas about education. 'You can forget your universities and your public schools,' Dixon was implying; 'I learned mathematics miles away from any of them.'

Dixon's gruff assertion might have offended his interviewers, and even lost him the transit of Venus job, but it may be that Dixon guessed that such a remark might have made him a more attractive prospect. He may have seen that they wanted a down-to-earth man, a good practical surveyor, who could act as a counter-balance to Charles Mason, who was first and foremost an astronomer.

Dixon's pit-cabin remark might also have been calculated to

make him appear honest. Honesty would be an essential qualification for anyone undertaking a mission to observe a transit of Venus, as a dishonest astronomer might have been tempted to fake his results, because in this case authentic results would be difficult, if not impossible, to come by.

And the crack about Cockfield Fell might have assured the Royal Society that, as a man straight up from the country, Dixon wouldn't be likely to challenge Charles Mason's authority as leader of the expedition, as might have been the case if Jeremiah had been, for instance, a London *savant* with aristocratic connections.

Modern psychology tells us that interviews are almost entirely useless as a way of winnowing out candidates for a job, not least because so much depends on the first impressions gleaned when the candidate first appear (which is why, all other things being equal, tall, good-looking people tend to do better in interviews).

It may be that Dixon secured the job as soon as the representatives of the Royal Society got a look at him, because he appeared young and strong. The trip to Sumatra which was the Royal Society's Plan A would have been extremely risky and arduous, even in peace-time.

Dixon used his size and strength in a most un-Quakerly way, on one occasion in Philadelphia, when he took up arms in defence of a black female slave. 'Thou must not do that!' he cried when he saw a white man whipping her, using the typical 'thou' of Quaker plain speech.

'You be d....d! Mind your own business,' the white man replied.

'If thou doesn't desist I'll thrash thee!' said Dixon, seizing the man's whip and proceeding to thrash him, as he had promised. He took the whip home as a souvenir, and this very whip was shown at an exhibition about Dixon at the Bowes Museum in County Durham in 2013.

Dixon's map of the Line, and a replica crown marker stone at Cockfield, showing the Penn coat of arms

William Johnson, the 'Mohawk Baronet'

Locomotive named for Dixon in 2013. Photos by Robert Jones

Dixon's brother George, and Bishop Auckland native, instrument-maker John Bird

Blue plaque on Garden House, Cockfield,
and view of Cockfield village green

Cockfield Fell. Generations of Dixons owned a coal-mine here

V. Transatlantic

By the time the job that was to write Dixon and Mason into American history was offered to them, Charles and Jeremiah had become celebrities, celebrated for the value, completeness and accuracy of their observations at the Cape.

In effect, they were called in as scientists to solve a scientific problem that had defeated the local experts – they were tasked with determining and marking the correct location of the border between Pennsylvania and Maryland. At the time, these areas were not American states in the modern sense, but provinces ruled from Britain.

The border between these two provinces needed to be definitively marked out so that people living near the boundary would know what province they were in, to whom they were supposed to pay taxes and rent, and whose laws they were supposed to obey.

Although the results of Dixon and Mason's efforts are called 'the Mason-Dixon Line' or 'Mason and Dixon's Line', by the time their work was finished in 1767, they had actually marked out several lines, as the first simplified map printed at the end of this chapter clearly shows (the map is from the online version of the National Atlas of the United States).

The map seems to show two lines – the longest is the horizontal line, which Dixon and Mason surveyed from east to west. This is called the 'West Line', and the Englishmen intended this to accurately follow a line of latitude. It is made clear on the diagram that Dixon and Mason didn't finish their line: they stopped before they reached the westernmost extent of Pennsylvania.

The near-vertical line on the map first map below is called the Tangent Line, and this was supposed to run from a point below the eastern end of the West Line to a point midway along the east-west line that crosses the Delmarva peninsular, the northeast section of which is marked 'DE' for 'Delaware'. In 1763, when Dixon and Mason started their work, Delaware was part of Pennsylvania.

What you can't really see on the map is the so-called North Line, which leads from the eastern end of the West Line to the beginning of the Tangent Line. You can, however, see the curved line that runs from the top of the point where the North Line and the West Line meet. This is a section of a circular line drawn around the port town of New Castle, Pennsylvania. The Pennsylvanians wanted this town to be included in their province because it gave them access to the sea.

The second picture below, by Lucas Snyder, is a diagram of the area where the West and North Lines meet the line drawn around New Castle.

To mark out the North Line and the Tangent Line, Dixon and Mason employed axemen to cut a broad 'visto' through the trees and other flora that lay in their path. Charles Mason described how he could usually see for about two miles along this cleared area, and how in the distance it was 'beautifully terminating to the eye in a point', a reference to the effect of perspective.

The fact that they had created this 'visto', like a fire-break in a forest, through miles of flattish country, gave the Englishmen an idea. It occurred to them that they now had an opportunity to measure the length of a degree of latitude: this would be the distance along the surface of the earth of one of those ninety degrees of northern latitude that stretch from the north pole down to the equator. In 1768, after Native American wars had forced them to abandon work on their West Line, the surveyors would return east to measure their degree of latitude.

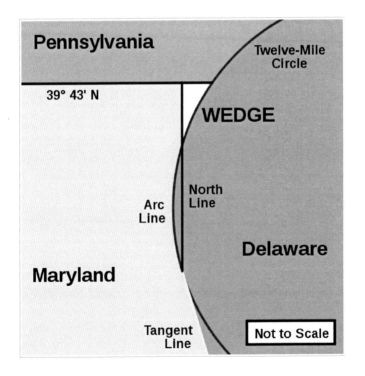

27

VI. How They Did It

Although they were by no means the first in the field, and although their work is now known to be inaccurate, Dixon and Mason set new standards of accuracy as they surveyed their lines, and went to great lengths to overcome the serious technical difficulties which had defeated previous attempts to survey them.

What Dixon and Mason had to do with their West Line was to make an imaginary line, of latitude, into a real line made visible by specially-made stone markers.

The method the Englishmen used involved regular checks of their own latitude, to find out how far they had drifted off the true east-west line of latitude, if at all.

Lines of latitude are the horizontal black lines that run across maps, and wrap themselves around model globes of the earth, parallel to the equator. They are not equally spaced in terms of distances across the surface of the planet – theoretically, they are angles measured from the centre of the earth.

If Dixon and Mason's procedure depended on regular checks on their latitude, then how did they check it? The answer lies in the most useful instrument they took with them, the zenith sector or zenith telescope. Made by County Durham man John Bird, the Englishmen's zenith sector instrument was so large, delicate and valuable that it had to be carried in a cart on a feather-bed through the American wilderness.

The actual zenith sector Dixon and Mason used was destroyed in a fire in 1897. The picture printed at the end of this chapter shows a similar instrument (on the right) made by David Rittenhouse and used by Rittenhouse and Andrew Ellicott to complete Dixon and Mason's survey, in 1784. The instrument on the left is an equal altitude instrument, made by Ellicott, similar to the one used by Dixon and Mason. This was used for some of the tasks that were carried out with the zenith sector, but it was more suitable for observing objects that were lower in the sky.

In theory, Dixon and Mason's sector could point straight up to the zenith (directly above their heads) because its telescope could be lined up with the plumb-line that was part of its mechanism (part of the plumb-line is visible in the picture). With the sector in this position, the Englishmen could watch for particular stars to cross their meridian (the imaginary line of longitude that ran from the north to the south pole, right over their position).

They had tables, published by the Royal Observatory, that told them when certain stars would cross this meridian. The tables also gave them figures for how high in the sky these stars would be at that time: these heights were expressed as degrees north, just like the degrees of latitude on the earth, in the northern hemisphere.

One of the stars Dixon and Mason used to find their latitude was Delta Persei. The latitude of this star on the imaginary celestial sphere is forty-seven degrees and thirty-nine point seven minutes. From their point of view, Delta Persei crossed their meridian over seven degrees to the north. The duo subtracted this amount from the known 'declination' of the star to find their own latitude – in other words, how far south they were from where they would have to be for Delta Persei to pass right over their heads. From this procedure, they discovered that the line of north latitude they had to follow was thirty-nine degrees, fifty-six minutes and twenty-eight seconds north.

They had been instructed to start their West Line at a latitude fifteen miles south of what was then the southernmost house in

29

the city of Philadelphia: a house on Cedar Street. They knew that if they measured directly south from Philadelphia, they would end up having to cross the River Delaware several times, so they proceeded thirty-one miles west and set up a marker (now a monument called the Stargazer's Stone) on a plantation owned by one John Harland, in the January of 1764.

Having established the latitude of their temporary observatory at Harland's plantation, Dixon and Mason measured fifteen miles south to the latitude which their West Line was supposed to follow. They measured this distance with the special surveyor's chains they took with them, and checked their latitude by the stars.

Most of the Englishmen's astronomical observations would have been meaningless if they couldn't be screwed down to a particular time of day or night. The difficulty of ascertaining the correct time in those days was one of the problems that caused delays in Dixon and Mason's progress, and forced them to spend nearly five years in America.

Although they had a good pendulum clock, specially made by a Mr Jackson of Philadelphia, Dixon and Mason still needed to spend many hours observing the stars to build up raw data with which to determine the correct time of day, or night.

We have already seen how Dixon and Mason had to go to great lengths, during their time at the Cape, to determine exactly what time it was. This was because most of the clocks and watches of the time were not reliable, and in any case astronomers and other scientists didn't trust them, even if, like the celebrated clocks of John Harrison, they kept good time.

The figures the Englishmen obtained from the stars had to be painstakingly adjusted, using mathematics and a pen and paper, before they could become useful.

As well as problems with time, and other technical problems, the Englishmen had to put up with the vagaries of the weather.

They couldn't work at all in the winter months, and in spring and autumn they still had to contend with rain, and freezing temperatures. In summer, they were sometimes plagued by mosquitoes, and couldn't even line up their instruments because of shimmering heat.

18th Century zenith sector (right) and equal altitude instrument

VII. Indian Country

Another problem they met with between Pennsylvania and Maryland was more serious than any technical or meteorological difficulty, and might in fact have led to their violent deaths. In any case, it caused them to abandon their task before it was finished.

Dixon and Mason came to America in November 1763, nine months after the Seven Years' War had been brought to an official close by the Treaty of Paris, in February of the same year. As such, the Englishmen had a right to expect that the French and Indian War, as it was known in America, had ended. Unfortunately, this was not the case. The war had exacerbated many political problems in the New World, and, certainly from the Native American point of view, these issues could not be settled by the signing of some papers in a city nearly four thousand miles away. Both the Native Americans and the whites were perpetrating atrocities, and the further west they went, the more likely Dixon and Mason were to encounter trouble.

The most powerful Native American group in the area was the Iroquois alliance, or Six Nations of the Long House. This comprised the Mohawk, Oneida, Onondaga, Cayuga, Seneca and Tuscarora Nations, and it was felt that Dixon and Mason could not resume surveying the last sections of their West Line in 1767 unless they had the agreement of the Six Nations.

The man who negotiated this agreement was one of the most remarkable men of the age – the so-called 'Mohawk Baronet', William Johnson. Johnson was from an old Irish Catholic family that had changed its surname from Macshane, meaning 'son of Shane' to Johnson, meaning 'son of John'.

Like Dixon, William Johnson was a large, strong man, as can be seen from the Quaker artist Benjamin West's portrait of him. Both tended to wear red coats, but as a major-general in the British Army Johnson was probably obliged to at times.

In 1756 Johnson became British Superintendent of Affairs for the northern colonies, and as such he was an obvious choice to barter an agreement with the Six Nations to allow Dixon and Mason to complete the last stretch of their survey.

The agreement was necessary not only to assure the Englishmen that they wouldn't be attacked by Iroquois, but also because the natives regarded the land this far west as theirs by right, and were suspicious of surveyors working on it: might they not be making plans to build yet another white settlement?

In 1763, the year when Dixon and Mason started their survey, the British King George III had issued a proclamation insisting that no colonists should settle west of the Allegheny Mountains, which are part of the Appalachian mountain chain. But to get to the western end of Pennsylvania, Dixon and Mason had to go beyond the Alleghenies.

Although, thanks to Johnson's treaty, the survey could now go beyond the mountains, it proved to be impossible for the team to drag their marker-stones across such hilly country. They abandoned the sixty or so remaining stones at the foot of Sideling Hill (north-west of Hancock, Maryland) and proceeded to use wooden markers or piles of stones to mark their Line.

The stones they left behind were supposed to be placed every mile along their line, with fancier 'crown' stones every five miles. They were cut from Portland stone, a grey-white limestone from the island of Portland in the English Channel. They had been transported to America at great cost, and although some of the stones Dixon and Mason abandoned were stolen by local settlers to be incorporated into buildings, many were redistributed along the Line in the 1900s.

In 1767, the Englishmen re-started their work on the West Line near what is now the city of Cumberland in Maryland.

Part of the agreement with the Iroquois was that the alliance would supply Native American escorts to accompany the surveyors on the last stretch of their expedition. Fourteen Native Americans (three Onondagas and eleven Mohawks) turned up, together with the explorer, trader, friend of the natives and British Army veteran Hugh Crawford; in July 1767. Crawford himself was dressed in buckskins, Indian-style, and carried a large hunting-knife and a musket. The new additions swelled the expedition's numbers, so that now they proceeded west with as many as a hundred and fifteen men, more than twice as many as they had needed back east, when they started their survey.

This peaceful host consisted of, among others, five 'instrument carriers', a shepherd to guide the animals that followed the wagon train, a male 'milk maid', seven cooks, numerous tent-keepers, axe-men, chain-carriers (for the measuring chains), and pack-horse drivers.

Crawford, whose knowledge of the terrain and its natives was profound, warned the surveyors that there was war further west, between the Seneca and Cherokee Nations. The survey party was therefore well-advised to proceed with caution, or 'gan canny' as this is expressed in the Durham dialect. Part of this caution consisted of forbidding the men to go off on hunting expeditions to supplement their diet with fresh game.

Despite their guns, their numbers, their Native American escorts, the treaty with the Six Nations and the presence of Hugh Crawford, a feeling of uneasiness seems to have pervaded the last stretch of Dixon and Mason's survey, in 1767.

It seems that the surveyors and their escorts were fearful of an attack by the natives, even though they received several friendly visits from First Nations people as they neared the end of their

West Line. On the seventeenth of August they were visited by thirteen Delawares, 'one of them a Nephew of Captain Black-Jacobs'. Mason adds that 'this Nephew of Black-Jacobs was the tallest man I ever saw'.

One cause of uneasiness in this last stretch of Dixon and Mason's survey was the fact that nobody seemed to be sure exactly where they were supposed to stop. William Johnson's treaty meant that they could go beyond the Alleghenies, but how far beyond? At one point, Mason seems to have thought that they should stop at the westernmost edge of Maryland, although that is not as far west as the official western border of Pennsylvania.

On October the ninth, the party reached a Native American war-path, the Catawba. Beyond the Catawba path Dixon and Mason's native escorts refused to go. The survey had ended, about thirty-five miles short of the furthest western extent of Pennsylvania.

Dixon and Mason went a little beyond the Catawba Path to the top of Brown's Hill, where they set up their zenith sector and again asked the stars exactly where they were. There they were visited by an elderly native whom Mason identified as 'Prince Prisqueetom, Brother to the King of the Delawares'. This may have been Pisquatomen, the hot-tempered brother of the peacemaker-king Tamaqua; although in his essay on the brothers in a 1996 book called *Northeastern Indian Lives*, Michael N. McConnell insists that Pisquatomen would have been dead by this time.

On Brown's Hill Dixon and Mason drove a stake into the ground and piled a conical heap of rocks around it, that stood five feet tall. By this time they were further west than the westernmost point of Maryland, and their line had become the border between Pennsylvania and Virginia (now West Virginia).

VIII. Kvaløya

Jeremiah Dixon's work for the proprietors of Pennsylvania and Maryland was nicely bracketed by work for the Royal Society, observing transits of Venus. Having arrived back in England in the October of 1768, by half-past ten in the morning of May the seventh 1769 Dixon was on a frigate called the *HMS Emerald* (thirty-two guns) 'anchored in Hammerfost-Bay, near the town of Hammerfost, on Hammerfost-Island'.

In fact Dixon had arrived at the town of Hammer*fest* on the Norwegian island of Kvaløya. He was there to observe the 1769 transit from a latitude far enough north for the whole thing to be seen when the sun was already high in the sky. In theory, this would be better than Dixon and Mason's experience at Cape Town, and Maskelyne's on St Helena in 1761, when the transit had already started before the sun rose in those places.

Indeed at Hammerfest on June the third, when Dixon was to observe his last transit of Venus, the sun would have been up all day. This 'midnight sun' might have been disorientating for the County Durham man, as there is no place in England, even in the far north, where the sun doesn't go down at night, even in high summer. Visitors from nearer the equator, arriving in places where the midnight sun is seen, can suffer from insomnia and depression as a result of it.

At Hammerfest, Dixon was in sole charge of the expedition, Charles Mason having been sent to observe the transit from Cavan in County Donegal, Ireland. 1769 would be the last time anyone would be able to observe a transit of Venus for over a century, until 1874, and scientists were out in force all over the world, hoping for clear weather.

Although Dixon had been posted to a place from which the entire transit could have been visible, his excitement over this prospect might have been tempered by the harsh conditions at Hammerfest, and the difficulty of the terrain.

After more than two weeks, Dixon seemed to have pretty much everything ready for the transit, when the weather took a turn for the worse and a 'violent storm of wind, hail and snow' set in, which continued for nearly a week. Dixon must have been concerned that the storm would continue right through the transit.

As soon as the clouds cleared, however, Dixon was observing the movements of the sun again, and he was able to do so on the three days before the transit itself.

When the transit of Venus finally happened, on June the third, clouds prevented Dixon from seeing it for longer than a few minutes, although the whole thing would have lasted more than six hours, from early in the afternoon to early evening.

Two days after the elusive transit, everything was back on board the *Emerald*, and Dixon was ready to leave.

XI. Home to Cockfield

Although Jeremiah Dixon may have been able to establish himself as a successful surveyor in many places including London, Pennsylvania, or even South Africa, where his fame as a scientist would surely have drawn clients to him, 'Jerry the Astronomer' (as later generations of Dixons would call him) preferred to return to the village of Cockfield in County Durham.

When he drew up a will in 1778, the year before his death, Dixon left his 'copyhold houses, garth, garden, and premises within the manor of Bondgate in Auckland' to his 'good friend John Raylton and his heirs Upon Trust and for the benefit of Margaret Bland'.

What Dixon had evidently got his 'good friend' to agree to do, before he drew up his will, was to look after his 'premises' at Bondgate in Auckland and to ensure that 'any profits becoming due from these premises shall go towards the maintenance of the two daughters of the said Margaret Bland, namely, Mary and Elizabeth, until 21'. At twenty-one, the girls would inherit Dixon's copyhold (an ancient kind of lease).

Everything else in Dixon's will was left to his brother Ralph and his sister Elizabeth, but there is no suggestion that Margaret Bland was also a relative. These details have led some to suspect that Margaret was Jeremiah's mistress, and that her daughters Mary and Elizabeth were their illegitimate children.

In any case, Elizabeth and Margaret lived long enough to inherit the Auckland 'premises' and to sell off the dye-house in 1822, for ninety pounds – the equivalent of about four thousand pounds, or over six and a half thousand US dollars today.

Jeremiah Dixon died on the twenty-third of January 1779, and was buried in the Quaker burial ground at Staindrop, which is now part of the garden of a private house. Somehow Jeremiah and his brother George, a well-to-do mine-owner, were able to be buried in the Quaker way though both had been disowned by the Raby Quaker meeting: Jeremiah was disowned in 1760 for excessive drunkenness and keeping 'loose' company.

Though the family house at Cockfield still survives, the meeting house and Quaker burial ground at Raby perished when the whole village was torn down early in the nineteenth century: the land it stood on is now part of the park around Raby Castle. The nearest Quaker meeting that still survives is at Bishop Auckland; a small meeting that only meets once a month. Neither the Bishop Auckland Quakers or those at Durham have their own meeting-house.

The site of Dixon's body cannot now be located with any certainty, but his name lives on in the name of the line he marked out with Charles Mason. The greatest significance of the Mason-Dixon Line lay in its status, not just as the dividing line between Pennsylvania and Maryland, but also as the boundary between the South, where slavery continued until Abraham Lincoln's Emancipation Proclamation of 1863, and the North, where virtually all slaves were free by 1840.

As well as helping to mark its northern boundary, Jeremiah Dixon may have given the South its nickname – 'Dixie', although this term began to be used a long time after his death. The name may, however, be a reference to a ten-dollar bill that circulated in the South, which had the French word 'dix' on it. Such notes certainly existed: they were issued by the Citizens State Bank in New Orleans, and they had to have French on one side because many of the citizens of Louisiana were more at home with the French language than they were with English.

Further Reading

Danson, Edwin: *Drawing the Line: How Mason and Dixon Surveyed the Most Famous Border in America*, Wiley, 2001

Ecenbarger, William: *Walkin' the Line: A Journey from Past to Present Along the Mason-Dixon Line, Evans*, 2000

Furneaux, Rupert: *The Seven Years War*, Granada, 1973

Grumet, Robert S. (ed.): *Northeastern Indian Lives, 1632-1816*, University of Massachusetts Press, 1996

Jones, Rufus: *The Quakers in the American Colonies*, Norton, 1966

Kenny, Kevin: *Peaceable Kingdom Lost: The Paxton Boys and the Destruction of William Penn's Holy Experiment*, Oxford, 2009

Laver, James: *Costume and Fashion: A Concise History*, Thames and Hudson, 1982

Longstaff, George Blundell: *The Langstaffs of Teesdale and Weardale: Materials for a History of a Yeoman Family*, M. Hughes and Clarke, 1923

Parkman, Francis: *The Conspiracy of Pontiac and the War after the Conquest of Canada*, Little, Brown, 1922

Peacock, Jonathan: *Jeremiah Dixon: Scientist, Surveyor and Stargazer*, The Bowes Museum, 2013

Pynchon, Thomas: *Mason & Dixon*, Jonathan Cape, 1997

Raistrick, Arthur: *Quakers in Science and Industry*, David and Charles, 1968

Rutherford, Moira: *Quakers in the City of Durham 1654-1858*, White & Co., 1997

Sobel, Dava: *Longitude*, Fourth Estate, 1995

Stein, Mark: *How the States got their Shapes*, Harper, 2008